JENNY'S SPOOKY LITTLE TALES: VOL. 3

Compiled by Jenny Floyd

I0158213

Nightmare Press
Shepherdsville, KY

Edited by Jacob Floyd

Cover by Christy Aldridge of Grim Poppy Design

In memory of Renee Good and Alex Pretti, murdered for speaking out and standing up to injustice during dangerous times. America will not forget you, and the good guys will mourn you, for you were both on the right side of history.

Other works by Jenny Floyd

Jenny is the Strange and Unusual
Death and Lipstick

With Jacob Floyd

Haunts of Hollywood Stars and Starlets
Aliens Over Kentucky
Strange and Unusual Mysteries
Be Our Ghost
Kentucky's Strange and Unusual Haunts
Kentucky's Haunted Graveyards

JENNY'S SPOOKY LITTLE TALES: VOL. 3

Compiled by Jenny Floyd

INTRODUCTION

——————⬤——————

Over the years, we have written many books on the paranormal. For some, we conducted extensive studies firsthand, and for others, simply researched existing archives and spoken to many people. Our first three books—*Louisville's Strange and Unusual Haunts, Kentucky's Haunted Mansions,* and *Indiana's Strange and Unusual Haunts*—have been out of print for several years. We intend to add new stories we have discovered to these tomes in the future, and republish them with Nightmare Press.

In the meantime, Jenny has decided to compile ten more of her favorite stories spanning the decade we have dedicated to paranormal research, as well as researching that which is strange and unusual. For this third installment, she has even included work from her memoirs and *Death and Lipstick.* These stories have been re-edited and expanded in accordance with whatever might have changed. We hope those of you who have followed our work over the last ten years enjoy this little collection; and we hope those of you who are new to our work decide to join our other followers.

Thank you for ten years of support, and here's to many more,

Jacob and Jenny Floyd

The Frightening Floyds

F. SCOTT FITZGERALD
AND
THE SEELBACH HOTEL

(from *Haunts of Hollywood Stars and Starlets*)

L ouisville natives who are into the paranormal know the ghost stories about the Seelbach Hotel. Its history is rich and sketchy; classy and criminal; elegant and eerie, and many people have made various claims of experiencing paranormal activity within it. The hotel is also the final stop on a local ghost tour called the Louisville Ghost Walk. There is also a night manager there who can tell you all the haunted comings and goings he has heard about and witnessed for himself, if you can catch him on the right night. We too had our own experiences there and wrote about them in our first book, *Louisville's Strange and Unusual Haunts*. Off and on, we visit the hotel, just for fun, and to see if we can dig up anymore ghost tales. We also like to ask about the history and some of the famous names that stayed there in the past.

One of our favorite occupants from days gone by is novelist F. Scott Fitzgerald, who wrote many jazz-age novels and short stories about the opulence and excess that prevailed in the Roaring Twenties. Though he often lived in the shadow of friend and contemporary Ernest Hemingway, many rank him among the greatest novelists of his generation.

His time spent in Louisville inspired his iconic novel, *The Great Gatsby*. Even more specifically, the novel's "Muhlbach Hotel," took inspiration from the Seelbach Hotel. Though Fitzgerald never confirmed this, the similarities are certainly there, and it is known that he spent time at Louisville's Camp Zachary Taylor while he was in the army. During that period, he spent a lot of time visiting the Seelbach, and some say that's where he got significant inspiration for the novel.

He wasn't a Hollywood star. but his work influenced Hollywood films, with five film adaptations of *The Great Gatsby* made: 1926, 1949, 1974, 2000 (made-for-TV), and 2013. *The Beautiful and Damned* was adapted to film in 1922, *Tender is the Night* in 1962, television in 1985, and stage by The Fountain Theatre in 1995; and his unfinished novel, *The Last Tycoon*, was adapted to numerous media and entertainment outlets with the most notable being the 1976 film starring Robert DeNiro. His 1922 short story, "The Curious Case of Benjamin Button" was adapted to film in 2008, starring Brad Pitt. It was both a commercial and critical success and won three of the thirteen Academy Awards nominations it received: Best Art Direction, Best Makeup, and

Best Visual Effects. So, even if Fitzgerald himself was not a Hollywood name, his work gained enough success in Tinseltown to earn him a spot in its legacy.

Francis Scott Key Fitzgerald, named after his second cousin, Francis Scott Key (another man with family ties to Kentucky), the man who wrote the "Star Spangled Banner," was born on September 24th, 1896 in Saint Paul, Minnesota to a well-to-do, upper-middle class family. Fitzgerald experienced a comfortable upbringing and attended some of the finest schools, including Princeton. Early in life he decided to become a writer and spent much of his time honing that craft. His severe dedication led to his grades suffering, which landed him on academic probation. He dropped out of college soon after and joined the Army.

Louisville's local lore says that during Fitzgerald's time stationed at Camp Zachary Taylor, he would visit the Seelbach Hotel to enjoy one of his favorite pastimes: drinking. Often, he would go down to the Bavarian-style bar in the hotel's basement, called the Rathskeller, and enjoy cigars and premium Kentucky bourbon. One evening, his unruly drunkenness forced staff to restrain and remove him from the hotel.

The innovative hotel left an impression on him. A lot of the speculation about Louisville's influence on *The Great Gatsby* comes with solid evidence. In fact, it is almost a certainty. Jay Gatsby, the title character, trained at Camp Zachary Taylor and fell in love with a southern Louisville socialite, Daisy Fay, who married another man in the Grand Ballroom of the "Muhlbach" Hotel (one of the Seelbach's main attractions is the Grand Ballroom on the 10th floor). Gatsby himself mirrors former Cincinnati prohibition gangster, George Remus, whom Fitzgerald met during his time in Louisville. It's hard to really debate the significant influence the author's time spent at the Seelbach had on his most famous work, which also stands as one of the most acclaimed literary novels of all time.

After his time in Louisville, Fitzgerald was at Fort Leavenworth, where he became a student to Dwight Eisenhower—a man he openly did not like. He went next to Alabama, stationed at Camp Sheridan outside Montgomery, as a Second Lieutenant. He never saw the war, though, as it ended in 1918 before his deployment.

While in Alabama, he met Zelda Sayre, the young daughter of a Supreme Court Justice. She became the object of his adoration, but he found himself rejected by her because he did not make enough to support her. His writing efforts had yet to turn out any success, so he went back home to New York and found menial jobs while continuing to work on his writing career. When *The Romantic Egotist* was accepted for publication and renamed *This Side of Paradise*, the novel was an instant success, gaining Fitzgerald an income substantial enough to convince his beloved Southern Belle to accept his hand in marriage.

The 1920s saw success and hardship for the Fitzgeralds. They spent a lot of time in Europe, and F. Scott befriended Ernest Hemingway. Their relationship had its difficulties, and Hemingway did not like Zelda. In his memoir, *A Moveable Feast*, Hemingway described Zelda as being insane and often blamed her for Fitzgerald's inability to complete novels in a timely fashion; he also accused her of driving his friend to drink so much, which distracted him from his novels and forced him to write commercial short-fiction for magazines—an act he derided.

F. Scott Fitzgerald did have a brief stint in Hollywood in 1926. He wrote flapper comedies for United Artists. During this time, he began his affair with Lois Moran, a television, film, and stage actress who became the inspiration for one of his main characters in *Tender is the Night*—Rosemary Hoyt. This situation put further strain on his and Zelda's marriage, so they left Hollywood after only a couple of months.

Despite the legacy F. Scott Fitzgerald left in the literary world, *This Side of Paradise* was his only novel that sold well. The remainder of his career was a constant financial struggle trying to support him and Zelda's lavish New York lifestyle, as well as her medical bills.

In 1930, Zelda's schizophrenia diagnosis confirmed Hemingway's suspicions about her sanity with her diagnosis of schizophrenia. Her health, which was already fragile, only worsened from thereon. In 1936, her ever-increasing violence caused Fitzgerald to have her committed to Highland Hospital in Asheville, North Carolina.

Despite his disdain for film work, Fitzgerald entered into a contract with Metro-Goldwyn-Mayer in 1937 because he needed the money. He moved to Hollywood and stayed there until his heart-attack death in 1940 at the age of forty-four. Since he was not a practicing Catholic, the Roman Catholic Church would not permit his burial at the Fitzgerald family plot in St. Mary's Cemetery in Rockville, Maryland, so he was buried in Rockville Union Cemetery instead. In 1975, his daughter, Scottie, had his and Zelda's remains moved to the St. Mary's family plot.

In the later years of his life, he thought of himself as a Hollywood hack, and mocked himself as such in his Pat Hobby short stories. Already an alcoholic, this poor self-image only worsened his disease. Poor F. Scott Fitzgerald, the doomed genius, had only two options: sell out or starve. Maybe this regret is what has him allegedly hanging around the famed hotel where his initial inspiration began, and where he had dreams of one day being a celebrated novelist.

There are many well-known haunts inside the Seelbach Hotel. F. Scott Fitzgerald is not one of them, as we never heard of his ghostly present during our initial research. In fact, we came upon this story simply by chance. Often, people ask us what we feel are some of the most haunted places we've visited. Naturally, as Louisville natives, people often seek our opinions about Waverly, which we place on that list. Other locations are the Old Stone Jail in Shepherdsville, Kentucky, Eastern Cemetery in Louisville, and the Seelbach Hotel.

Upon mentioning the Seelbach once to a man, Jacob ended up in a conversation about the many haunts reported there. Of course, we discussed the well-known accounts: The Lady in Blue, the waiters in the Ballroom, the strange hissing black mist on the 10th floor, as well as some of our own personal experiences. The man then told us that while he worked there long ago, he saw the ghost of F. Scott Fitzgerald a few times. We hadn't heard this one yet, so Jacob asked him to elaborate.

It appears the risqué 1920s author haunts the Rathskeller, having a smoke and a drink. He also walks from one side of the room towards the bar. The man telling us the stories claimed to see this image himself, along with a co-worker or two. When Jacob asked him if he was sure the spirit in question was

Fitzgerald, the man said he was certain of it, as he was a lifelong fan and "would know that man's face anywhere."

He also said Fitzgerald lingers in one of the doorways to the Grand Ballroom, nervously checking his watch. He doesn't know what this residual image could signify; he just knows it was him. He also claims to have encountered the famous specter wandering into Gatsby's on 4th. Obviously, this would not have been the name of the restaurant during F. Scott's days in Louisville, but maybe this one is an intelligent spirit allowing his romantic ego to propel him towards an establishment which carries his name.

We followed up on the man's paranormal claims and did not uncover any other witnesses. No one, at this time, that we know of, has spotted the ghost of F. Scott Fitzgerald wandering about the hotel. That doesn't mean he's not there, however. In the man's defense, he did say he was a lifelong fan of the writer, and that could have been the reason he recognized him. Who's to say someone else hasn't seen the legendary author's ghost but had no idea who it was? People that report spirits at the Seelbach might see F. Scott Fitzgerald all the time without recognizing him. We intend to continue asking around about this claim in hopes of finding out some new evidence that can confirm this story.

MARILYN MONROE
(from *Death and Lipstick*)

How would you like it if those tending to the corpse of someone you loved stood over her, openly critiquing her appearance for others to hear, saying she didn't take care of herself in the weeks before her death?

As someone who once worked in that industry, I can say it is sadly very common. I'm of the opinion if someone enters the death industry, they're supposed to have a sense of humanity. What I can't understand is how a funeral director can auction off someone's hair and falsies for their chest. How is this even allowed?

These are just a few things that happened to Marilyn Monroe after her sudden death in 1962. But wait, it gets darker. After Marilyn was long interred, Westwood Village Memorial Park Cemetery sold a mausoleum plot to a man who wished to have his body placed above Marilyn's plot, with him facedown so he could "be on top of Marilyn forever." Sadly, they granted his wish.

Of course, the public treated Marilyn like a sex symbol her entire career. In 1953, when Hugh Hefner launched *Playboy*, he was able to obtain nude photographs of Monroe for the inaugural issue. The actress didn't pose for the magazine, however. These were photographs she posed for in 1949, prior to her stardom, because she needed money. They changed hands a few times before Hefner was able to purchase them. As scandalous as this might seem, it didn't have any sort of negative impact on Monroe's career. In fact, she eventually became friends with Hefner.

Although her marriage to baseball legend Joe DiMaggio was abusive, and that he was controlling and jealous, there still seemed to be love there. Marilyn's famous subway grate publicity stunt for *The Seven Year Itch* infuriated DiMaggio, and this led to their divorce.

Even during the divorce, Marilyn decided to continue her relationship with Joe, and cried in the courtroom. DiMaggio had a change of heart and began to continuously write love letters to Marilyn. Despite his tumultuous personality, DiMaggio's love for Marilyn seemed legitimate and strong. He never remarried.

After Monroe passed, along with Monroe's next-of-kin—her half-sister—DiMaggio made the funeral arrangements. In her hands, he placed the posy of pink tea cups he had gifted her and never left her casket during the proceedings.

DiMaggio sent a dozen roses to her plot three times a week for twenty years. Legend has it that, before he was about to die, he said, "I finally get to see Marilyn again."

For the funeral, Marilyn's personal makeup artist, Allen "Whitey" Snyder, did her makeup. Snyder had been with Monroe during most of her career, and they became very close friends. Not only did Snyder apply her makeup for the funeral, but he was also a pallbearer.

Due to the damage done to Marilyn during the autopsy, hairstylist Agnes Flanagan, who had worked with Monroe on a few films, most notably *Some Like It Hot*, brought the wig Monroe had worn on her final film, *Something's Got to Give*—which she was fired from and was never finished—and applied it for the services.

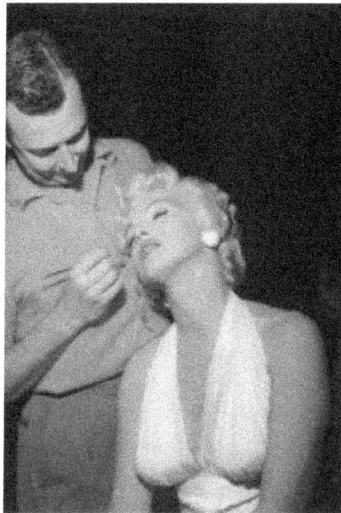

C onspiracy theories about Monroe's death began soon after her passing. In the 1964 pamphlet, *The Strange Death of Marilyn Monroe*, Frank A. Capell claimed Marilyn's death was part of a communist conspiracy. According to

Capell, many of Monroe's associates were communists, including her ex-husband Arthur Hiller. He also alleged Marilyn had an affair with then US Attorney General Robert F. Kennedy, who Capell said was a communist sympathizer. When Marilyn threatened to leak that information, according to Capell, RFK had her killed.

The affair with RFK allegation was furthered by Norman Mailer in *Marilyn: A Biography*. However, Mailer claimed Monroe was murdered either by the FBI or CIA as a way to put pressure on the Kennedys. During an interview with Mike Wallace, Mailer admitted he invented those allegations to ensure sales for his book, and that he believed her death was most likely an accidental overdose. There are those who remain skeptical, however, believing one of those government organizations got to Mailer, causing him to recant his accusations.

Shortly after, in 1975, a man by the name of Robert F. Slatzer claimed, in his book *The Life and Curious Death of Marilyn Monroe*, he had a three-day marriage to Marilyn in Mexico in 1952, and that they were friends up until her death. He also asserted Capell's claims were accurate. In doing so, he became a central figure for many Marilyn Monroe conspiracy theories.

The book *Who Killed Marilyn Monroe* added to these allegations, stating Marilyn kept a red diary with quite a bit of damning political information in it. The book also claimed that Monroe's home had been wiretapped by Bernard Spendel by order of Jimmy Hoffa, who was looking for evidence to use against the Kennedys.

Milo Speriglio's 1982 book *Marilyn Monroe: Murder Cover-Up* piled on to the ever-growing theory by stating that Hoffa had Chicago mafia don Sam Giancana murder the actress. According to the book, an employee at the Los Angeles cornoner's office said Marilyn's body had been beaten and bruised, but those details had been omitted from the report. The employee also claimed to have seen the elusive red diary.

M arilyn was discovered by photographer David Conover while shooting pictures of women working on war production assembly lines. None of her photographs were used, but this lead to her career as model.

Maryln also toured the war and gave many performance to American troops. She travled to Korea and performed in front of 100,000 soldiers in four days. She took time away from her honeymoon with Joe DiMaggio to do the tour.

Of course, being the ghost lady, you know I was going to talk about her ghost. It is believed she returns to our world at the Roosevelt Hotel in Hollywood, Califorinia. She lived there for two years before her modeling career took off. She also posed for the first ad of the hotel.

It is believed you can see her in a mirror in the hotel. A maid was dusting the mirror and saw the reflection of a sad-looking blonde woman. The maid turned to ask if she could help, but there was no one there.

The title of the book is *Death and Lipstick*. What if I tell you her favorite lipstick was not red, but she actually loved wearing orange and corals? Makeup compaines would work with big movie productions and send samples for her to wear. Her lipstick from Elizabeth Aren was a custom shade she wore, and it sold 65,000.

Lot #567 in **Sale** 3371 ICONS: PLAYBOY, HUGH
HEFNER, AND MARILYN MONROE
MARILYN MONROE | ELIZABETH ARDEN LIPSTICK

SOLD

WINNING BID
$65,000

MAYBE YOU CAN RELAX IN A HAUNTED HOUSE, BUT I CAN'T

(from *Jenny is the Strange and Unusual*)

Yes—I have lived in several haunted houses, but I don't know if they were exactly haunted, at least, not in the traditional sense. In the previous chapter, I discussed my theory about the spirits' possible connection to certain items or actions—and, that still may be the case. But, were they fully haunted? I'll explain what I mean.

I believe it is possible that these spirits live in a realm parallel to our own, which would mean they are always around, but not all can "pierce the veil." Those who can make up the traditional "haunts" we read or hear stories about, locations where many people, empathic or psychic, or not, experience paranormal encounters. Then there are those spirits who might not be able to easily reach our side and can only communicate through people who have those empathic abilities—that connection to the other side.

With my history of encountering the paranormal, I have begun to think sometimes, these spirits are drawn to me. I think the energy in those houses was reaching out to me for communication. I will further elaborate on some of the activity I discussed in the previous chapter.

I spoke about the communication with my grandfather on Plum Street. Though my mother was sitting outside, and our yard was not large, and he appeared to me there, she did not see him. Since I heard about the shooting that occurred on that property, I think that might have drawn my grandfather's spirit there. Was he there to protect? I don't know. I think spirits see me and know they can communicate with me, and that might be what led him to approach me.

I briefly discussed the activity in our house on West Third Street, and the tombstone taken from the "Forgotten

Cemetery." That cemetery, being a part of our tour, is alleged to be haunted. Two doctors—a father and son, named Ben and Henry Crist—often walk the grounds. Ben met his death by gunshot, and Henry's death happened mysteriously after the acquittal of his son's killer.

Also, there is a dark spirit there, walking the cul-de-sac behind the graveyard, where some have suggested there was once a small village predating even the historic area of Shepherdsville. There are different stories tied to this entity—a woman in a gray shroud heard and seen walking back there—and we did once capture a peculiar picture of a gray shape ducking among the shrubbery and tree limbs, after Jacob heard something walking heavily through the fallen autumn leaves.

Once, I was taking pictures of the graveyard on an overcast evening, with what looked to be a rainstorm approaching. Jacob took some pictures of the sky, and in one of the pictures we saw what looked to be the white face of a bearded man along the western fence-line. We later returned to the graveyard to debunk the image but found nothing in the vicinity to explain it.

We wonder if that's one of the doctors. One day, prior to knowing the story of the doctors, I was running the spirit box outside the cemetery, out by the grave-marker listing the known names of those interred there. I decided to run my finger down the list of names and ask if any spirits of the people listed were present. One quickly said, "Henry," and when I stopped running my finger along the list of names, I was pointing to Henry Crist.

Whatever the causes or explanations of these events, there has been a history of unexplained incidents there in the Old Pioneer Graveyard in First Street Park. So, with the presence of the tombstone near the house I grew up in, removed from the graveyard, it is quite possible it came attached with a restless spirit.

Some aggressive door slamming often occurred in the house. One night, I saw my bedroom door opening and called to my mother. When she went to see what the cause was, the door slammed hard right in front of her. I don't know if this was an angry spirit, or just someone trying to get our attention. If someone removed its tombstone from its resting place, that would be a good reason to be upset. Either way, it certainly got our attention.

The footsteps I mentioned before I believe could have been residual energy. Every night, at 2am, disembodied footsteps would leave the living room and go down the hallway into the kitchen. I remember my father sitting up late one night waiting to hear them. When two o'clock hit, the footsteps made their presence known, and he started hooting about it.

The steamboat table came to be our kitchen table due to my parents' love for antiques. The most vivid memory I can recall about that table is one day, feeling suddenly afraid, I began screaming at my mom that something was in the kitchen with us. Then, one of the chairs slid away from the table, as if someone had decided to excuse themselves. My mother then said, to whomever had moved the chair, "I'm sorry. Excuse me." Seems to be a little bit of Carol Ann activity from *Poltergeist*. At least the chairs didn't stack themselves on top of the table.

An incident I haven't mentioned is one involving a puppet named Charlie. He was a spooky doll, but nothing like Annabel, thankfully. He did move on his own sometimes. His body would shift, or his head would turn. That was always unsettling.

One night, after one of our tours, Jacob and I returned to the parking lot behind the funeral home where my house once stood. After experiencing the smell of tobacco that rode almost all the way home with us, we wanted to try the spirit box again. Something did call me "Little Jenny," which is something only family called me. I don't know if it was my grandfather, because, as I said, he never knew me in life, but he could have watched me as a spirit, and maybe he was trying to converse. Or, maybe it's just one of the resident specters repeating what they'd heard others say to me.

Once Jacob and I got into the paranormal, we did have some strange incidents in our apartment. Once, after watching a movie, I turned on the light, and both of us saw a black mist move on the stairs. I thought it ran down the steps, and he thought it went up the steps, but we both saw it. It reminded us both of a cat.

Another time, we were downstairs, and we heard a loud bang upstairs. Jacob went to investigate, but stopped at the bottom of the stairs because, when he turned the light on, he said he saw an unidentifiable misty figure on the steps. As he went up the stairs, he felt a cold draft, which was never present in our stairway because no breeze moved through there, especially from upstairs. When he reached the landing, he saw something knocked the spirit box off the second shelf of a small bookcase in the corner.

Was someone trying to speak to us?

MARIE LAVEAU

Portrait of Marie Laveau
(from *Strange and Unusual Mysteries)*

B orn in 1794, Marie Laveau was a Louisiana Creole known as the Voodoo Queen of New Orleans. Laveau healed the sick, rescued condemned men from the gallows, told fortunes, created potions and charms, and even conducted ceremonies in which the participants would become possessed by voodoo spirits known as loas.

A lot of information on Laveau exists, and much of it is fiction—either devised to enlarge her already massive personality, or fiction meant to smear her name. Separating the truth from the drama has been difficult for a lot of her fans. Following is an account we hope is as accurate as possible. Since most of what is known about the Voodoo Queen comes from oral tradition, it is quite difficult for anyone to say for certain how truthful every piece of information is. Hopefully, the information we have gathered is as close to the truth as it gets.

Laveau was born in the French Quarter on September 10th, 1794, an illegitimate daughter to a wealthy Creole plantation owner and his mistress. She grew up on her father's plantation, well educated, and a dedicated Catholic who attended mass every day. As she grew older, she became very beautiful: statuesque, tall, curly black hair, and golden skin. She attracted the attention of a freeperson from Haiti named Jacques Paris, and they were married. The St. Louis Cathedral in New Orleans has their preserved marriage certificate, documenting the names of Marie's parents.

In 1824, either by death or desertion, Paris was out of Laveau's life. She then began a career as a hairdresser and part-time nurse, until she entered a common-law marriage with Louis Christoph Dumesnil de Glapion, and began having children by him in succession. Dumesnil was wealthy, so Laveau ended her career to raise their fifteen children. During this period in her life, she became the Voodoo Queen.

Due to the Haitian Revolution of 1804, many Haitians in New Orleans revived the Voodoo religion; and although they often practiced it in the city, officials banned it at different times throughout history due to the sinister connotations people associated with this otherwise peaceful practice. Laveau began to learn the craft from a man calling himself Doctor John, and John Bayou. By 1830, Marie was one of many Voodoo Queens in the area.

Laveau's innovations eventually set her apart. She combined Voodoo with many Catholic traditions, such as holy water, incense, Christian prayers, and statues of saints. This combination made the practice of voodoo (the religion) and hoodoo (the magic associated with it) accepted by the upper-class of New Orleans. Laveau believed in spiritual forces that watch over the daily lives of their followers and can intervene when necessary. Some forces are kind while others are mischievous. One can establish bonds with these spirits through song, dance, music, and even by performing rituals with snakes.

Laveau began performing rituals at the Congo Square, one of the only areas in the segregated section of New Orleans where races could mix. At the Maison Blance—a house built specifically for voodoo rituals and rendezvous between black women and white men—Laveau also conducted operations selling gris-gris, charms, and magic powders able to cure certain ailments. She told fortunes, gave love advice, and would make custom gris-gris based on the customer's desired charms or hexes. Here she would grant wishes and help people destroy their enemies. Through these operations, she became the true Voodoo Queen of New Orleans.

Once she had overthrown the other queens, she began conducting business behind her cottage on St. Ann Street, performing exorcisms and giving sacrifices to spirits. Though some were critical of her, many feared her, while others revered her. To some, she was a practitioner of black magic and wielder of dark powers, while others thought of her as a saint for humanitarian work—the latter being more accurate.

Ultimately, Laveau retired in 1875, though she continued her humanitarian work with the poor and imprisoned while still offering readings at her home. It was her performing career that was over, as she sought a quieter life. She passed away peacefully on June 18th, 1881 and was buried in the St. Louis Cemetery #1 in the Laveau-Glapion family crypt. The crypt is aboveground, as required in New Orleans due to the water levels.

Laveau's tomb attracts the most visitors each year. Another crypt in Cemetery #2, known as the "Wishing Vault" or "Voodoo Vault," attracts those who hope Laveau will grant their wishes, and they illegally draw "xxx" on it to attract her spirit. They also draw pentagrams, hearts, and write poetry and their initials on the white slab. Even today, her impactful legacy lives on as thousands make the pilgrimage to her burial site each year to pay respects and ask for favors. The legend of the great Marie Laveau may never fade, no matter how much of it remains a mystery.

THE LOUISVILLE ALIEN:
SPRING-HEELED JACK

(from *Aliens Over Kentucky*)

When most people think of London murders, Jack the Ripper is the madman who comes to mind. While the Whitechapel serial killer is by far the most notorious, there are legends of another London lunatic that have grabbed the imaginations of folklorists. This killer predates the Ripper, and his name is also Jack. Just as elusive but even more bizarre, many believe this terror to be more than a man, but some sort of monster who breathed fire and could leap over buildings. They called him Spring-heeled Jack.

Sightings of Jack began in the late 1700s. According to a letter written to the *Sheffield Times* in 1808, Jack had been bouncing around the streets of London for many years. In 1837, a man walking one night claimed he saw a muscular man with pointed ears and glowing red eyes easily leap a cemetery fence and land directly in front of him. Not long after this incident, a woman named Polly Adams was found in the street with her blouse ripped from her body. She described a man with the same appearance accosting her, tearing off her blouse, and touching her with cold, corpse-like hands. These are unofficial reports.

Officially, Jack's first sighting was in 1837 when he attacked Mary Stevens while she walked along Cut Throat Lane on her way to Lavender Hill. As she was returning from a visit to her parents at Battersea, a tall, dark man leaped from the shadows, wrapped his arms around her, and kissed her wildly. As she struggled against him, he laughed hysterically. When she screamed, the attacker leapt away.

It is rumored that the following evening, the same man jumped into the middle of the road and caused an approaching carriage to veer off its path. He then bound over a nine-foot wall without touching it and vanished into the night. A few days later, police arrived at a scene where Jack had been spotted, and they found very deep ruts in the mud, as if someone had jumped from a great height. They noticed the impression on the ground suggested there was some kind of gadget attached to the heel. This supposed account has led to the theory that Jack was a man with springs on his shoes.

There were many more sightings over the next few years. Jack was accosting women, smacking men around, causing traffic issues, and inciting fear and hysteria in the populace. His legend was growing and developing all manners of odd descriptions. Some said this leaping man had bat-like wings, wore a cape, was pale and ghost-like, attacked them with long claws, and hands as hard as steel, before jumping away high into the night. Some speculated that he was a ghost while others claimed he was a shape-shifting monster. Most people laughed these accounts off as being nothing more than ghost stories. Nonetheless, these reports earned him the name Spring-heeled Jack.

In February of 1838, the jumper struck again. Late in the evening, the doorbell rang at the home of a young woman named Jane Alsop. When Alsop opened the door, a cloaked man suddenly threw back his shroud to reveal white clothing that looked to be very tight oilskin. As strange as this incident was, it became even more bizarre when the man began to breathe blue and white fire at her face while slashing at her with razor-sharp claws. Alsop's sister rushed into the room and scared off the attacker before he inflicted any serious damage.

Authorities arrested and tried a man by the name of Thomas Millbank for the crime, but released him due to

Alsop's claim that her attacker was breathing fire, and Millbank, of course, could not do that. However, he police found him wearing white overalls, and police found that he had dropped a great coat and a candle outside the building.

Then eighteen-year-old Lucy Scales had her own encounter with the jumping mini-dragon while she was walking with her sister in Limehouse. A figure leaped at her from the shadows of a nearby alley and started breathing fire into her face. Lucy screamed and the attacker fled. This incident left Scales in fits for several hours.

Many more sightings of the mysterious assailant occurred over the next few decades. His description took on new qualities with each report, such as his high-pitched laughter and large black boots. Witnesses continued to marvel at his inhuman leaping ability. They said he could clear walls without touching them, jump upon roofs of large houses, and quickly travel across town by leaping from rooftop to rooftop.

Sightings became more widespread, even if they were less frequent. A report from Northamptionshire described him as having horns and red eyes. He allegedly started attacking mail coaches in East Anglia. He supposedly tossed a prostitute off a bridge in 1845, in front of several witnesses. We could find no details explaining why witnesses believed Jack perpetrated this act. Perhaps the assailant leapt into the air before tossing the prostitute into the water. In 1847, a man named Captain Finch was arrested for attacking two women while wearing a skin coat, skullcap, horns, and mask.

An interesting incident occurred in 1855 after a hard snowfall in London. Albert Brailsford, headmaster of Topsham School in Devon, woke on February 8th to the sight of hoof prints in the snow. However, upon closer examination, Brailsford found some very odd details about these prints. First, they appeared to come not from a quadruped, but something bipedal. The prints were only eight inches apart and appeared to be about four inches in diameter. It looked as though they were in a straight line, as if whomever made them had been hopping along. He said they looked branded into the snow, which would suggest something hot made them. From there, Brailsford and some of his friends decided to follow the tracks and see where they led. The prints stopped right in front of a large wall. The snow on top of the wall remained intact. It was as if the creator of the prints had jumped straight up over the wall.

The most sensational Jack account may have been in 1872, when reports claimed that he jumped down into a small squad of soldiers and slapped one of them in the face. This angered the soldier, so he took out his gun and shot Jack. Allegedly, the shot, though it connected, had no effect. In fact, it angered him. He then chased the soldiers around, spraying his blue and white flames at them. He stuck around for a few more days, pestering them with his antics. Eventually, a mob formed nearby and tried to capture him. He fled, and some of the people claimed to have shot him but to no avail. Jack kept running and spitting out fire before finally jumping to safety, out of sight. Not long after, there was a report that a couple of villagers had cornered Jack on a roof and shot him, but he leaped away unharmed.

England, it seems, is not the only nation terrorized by this bouncing boogeyman. In 1880, Spring-heeled Jack came to Louisville. On July 28th, 1880, a man described as a "tall, thin weirdo" appeared in what is now known as Old Louisville, attacking women on the streets.

Reports claim this person leapt through the streets, tearing clothes off women. Many witnesses alleged to have seen him, and described him as having superhuman leaping abilities, jumping over carriages and onto rooftops to avoid capture. Though this Jack did not have red eyes, horns, nor did he breathe fire, he did wear a cape, helmet, and had a light glowing from his chest. Jack bounded through Butchertown, as well, since one report stated he vanished behind some large haystacks after jumping over them. Some described Jack as having flown into Louisville on some machine that had peddles and propellers. According to the reports, he peddled his way through the dark skies of Downtown, shortly before and after these attacks occurred.

There has been much speculation as to whom and/or what Jack was through the years. Many people remain skeptical, believing Jack to have been nothing more than a common man with some very inventive methods of attack. The subsequent reports following the first two are likely copycats, others thought a product of mass hysteria. Some say Jack was a nobleman by the name of Henry Beresford, Third Marquis of Waterford, who passed away in 1859. Beresford was known as the "Mad Marquis" due to his drunkenness and wild behavior. The biggest problem with this accusation is that there is zero evidence linking him to the Jack incidents.

The counterpoint to the claim that Jack was human is that the leaping abilities would have been impossible in such times. Many decades later, Nazi paratroopers who put springs in their boot heels to achieve better jumping abilities all ended up with broken ankles. Skeptics then insist that the additional attributes that made Jack superhuman were imaginary. They argue his origins grew from stories about ghosts stalking the streets of London in the early 19th century. These "ghosts" were pale and humanlike, and they preyed upon those who walked the streets alone in the dark of night. These stories became a part of local lore, and some say that it is what gave rise to the myth of Spring-heeled Jack.

Those who believe his existence to be otherworldly have other theories. Some say he was a demon summoned into our world by occult practitioners. One of the most common explanations is that he was extraterrestrial. Many believe that the descriptions of Jack—the red eyes, pointy ears, the pale skin, the long, spindly claws, the ability to leap and breathe fire—point to him being a visitor from another planet.

Regarding the leaping ability, some think the creature, or creatures, we know as Spring-heeled Jack came from a planet with a higher gravity than ours, which gave him that extraordinary vertical. Those who subscribe to this theory also believe this could explain his high-pitched laughter. Since our atmosphere would have seemed thin to him, it very well could have made him dizzy and somewhat excited, which could have led to his riotous cackling and outlandish behavior. The eyes, they explain, could have been reflective due to him being from a darker planet where there is not as much light. His ability to breathe fire would have been either a bioelectric shock that his kind used to stun their victims, or some sort of phosphor lighted by his bioluminescence, which would explain why the perceived flames didn't burn anyone.

Accounts of Jack continued into the 20th century, across England and even into the states. In 1953, three Houston residents spotted a tall man in a black cape, skin-tight pants, and quarter-length boots leaping through town. They claim he jumped into a Pecan tree where he stayed in plain view for several minutes before a rocket-shaped UFO shot from across the street and took him away into the sky.

Naturally, there are those who say even these reports are fabrications, and that no one in the 1800s, save a few of the documented cases, ever reported encountering anyone like this. They say that while there were accounts stating a strange man was running around town accosting women, all the added sensationalism are embellishments that grew into a very colorful super-villain story.

There is no true evidence to support this explanation, and thus the believers keep believing. According to a few sources, Spring-heeled Jack did make his way to Old Louisville, and dubbed the Demon Leaper. Was this the same individual? Did he fly across the ocean to our little corner of the world and cause a stir? It's quite possible. It could have been a copycat, or it could not have happened at all.

Let's just say for a minute that at least most of these accounts are true, and that this strange being did find himself bouncing around the streets of Louisville, making unwanted advances on women. The alien theories are interesting points to consider. It could be why he had the gyroscope, if he did indeed have that. To the open-minded believer in the extraterrestrial, this is a fascinating possibility, and very intriguing addition to the encyclopedia of Kentucky alien encounters.

MINNIE'S GONE MISSING

(from *Kentucky's Haunted Graveyards*)

Located just down the road from North Bullitt High School and Hebron Middle School in northern Bullitt County is the small, but nice, Hebron Cemetery. Developed in 1894, Hebron Cemetery replaced the Old Pioneer Graveyard, or as we dubbed, the Forgotten Cemetery, from our book *Kentucky's Strange and Unusual Haunts*, as well as featured in the final chapter of *Kentucky's Haunted Graveyards*.

There are many people significant to Bullitt County history interred at Hebron Cemetery. However, the best-known person laid to rest there is actor, artist, and author Gardner McKay. Though McKay was born in New York City and died in Hawaii, he stayed a while in the Louisville area as his father and grandfather were from Covington, Shelbyville, and Louisville. Other family members of his had lived in both Bullitt and Nelson counties.

A Revolutionary War soldier named John Beckwith rests at Hebron Cemetery. He was the one who thought of building the old schoolhouse that once stood near the graveyard. Beckwith's original grave was in the Old Brooks Cemetery, later sold and relocated. The city moved Beckwith's body, along with those of his family, and their stones, to the Hebron Cemetery.

We have heard conflicting reports about Beckwith. Many articles and historical records state he is buried there. Some historians believe his body isn't there, just the stone, and that his body is still where the Brooks Cemetery was, which now has U of L Medical Center South standing on top of it. We do not know for certain, but we have visited the graves. They are very close together, so it's possible no one is in any of the Beckwith graves. It's also not hard to believe the city buried them close together and had the stones simply placed on top of the site, maybe not necessarily spaced out precisely.

As for haunts, there is a story of a woman who wanders around the graveyard at night, carrying a lantern among the rows of tombstones, looking to the trees for her cat. The woman is elderly, dressed in a long black dress and apron, with a covering over her head, as if protecting herself from a cold wind that blew the night she lost her pet. Some say she appears only on a night when the moon is full and bright in the sky, as an apparition in the moonlight. Others say she appears only for a few nights around Halloween, leaving people to believe this is why she appears in such attire. There are more conflicting accounts of her appearances, as some say she has appeared on random nights throughout the years. There are those who have reported seeing her at dusk, just as the sun slips behind the horizon; others say she appears right around midnight; lastly, her arrival allegedly coincides with three in the morning. If all of this is correct, this leads us to believe she truly appears at various times.

As the story goes, the woman appears somewhere near the center of the cemetery, her lantern light bobbing ominously in the darkness, moving towards the south end of the graveyard, gazing up into the sky, and into nearby trees, yelling for her cat. Some believe when she appears to be simply looking to the sky, her spirit is a checking trees once there, but now gone. She will search for a few minutes, calling her cat's name, before becoming frantic with concern.

There are those who have seen her searching and have approached her to help. Some accounts say she ignores them when they ask her if she's okay or needs help. She just keeps yelling, "Minnie! Minnie, where are you?" Witnesses have followed her for a few minutes, only for her to disappear into the shadows of the night.

Another story claims the lady will answer. This one is from where, we think, the description of her being elderly came. In this account, the witness approaches her and asks if she is okay. Instead of ignoring the other person, the woman turns to them, takes down her head covering, and says, "I'm looking for my cat, Minnie. Have you seen a black cat around here?" Once the person tells her no, the woman resumes her search and vanishes.

There have been reports of a light floating through the graveyard and near the trees, without the presence of the woman. The light is large, orb-like, but with small beams radiating from the center. It travels around the center of the cemetery to the south end before vanishing. We suspect this happens when the woman's apparition cannot fully form, but the light is still present.

Minnie, it seems, might be present in Hebron Cemetery. People have reported hearing a disembodied cat meow towards the center of the cemetery, even possibly in the trees. The cat meows are somewhat urgent, but none can see the cat.

There have also been reports of a black cat seen walking across tombstones in the center of the cemetery. When approached, she meows, jumps down, and vanishes. There is a tale that Minnie runs from behind the stone towards the south end of the cemetery, disappearing in the sea of tombstones.

A black cat walks across the fence at the southern end of Hebron Cemetery. Whenever someone shines their flashlight on it, it looks towards them, meows, and vanishes. Another story places Minnie in a tree at the center of the graveyard. Someone wandering the paths will hear a meow, look up, and see the black cat there in the tree. If they look away for a second, the cat will be gone when they look back, never to spotted climbing down the tree, on any other branches, or down on the ground.

Of course, it's easy to explain these occurrences with the cat. It's a black cat in a graveyard at nighttime, surrounded by tombstones and trees. It could easily flee without notice. The cat could hide behind the stones, climb higher into the trees, or run away so swiftly no one spots it before it finds a crevice in which it can squeeze.

There is one story, though, much more difficult to explain. A couple visiting the grave of a family member, and there to see the Revolutionary War graves, said they were there close to sundown. As they approached the middle of the graveyard, they heard a cat meowing, as if in need of help. They looked around for a few minutes, unable to find it, even though it kept meowing. Eventually, they saw it in a tree. The woman called to the cat, but it wouldn't come down. They decided it must be okay, so they went to leave, as it was getting dark.

As they were leaving the cemetery, they heard a meow behind them. They turned to see the cat following them to their car, parked close to the entrance. The woman moved to pick the cat up, but it backed away, so she went towards the car. When she sat down, the cat came up to her and meowed. So, she let it jump on her lap. She asked her fiancé if they could take the cat home, since it didn't have a collar or anything to indicate it was someone's pet. Reluctantly, he agreed. As they drove towards the exit, the cat became apprehensive and meowed, with its eyes wide. Just as they were about to pass through the exit, the cat meowed again and suddenly jumped into the backseat. When the woman turned around to see what it was doing, the cat was no longer there. The back windows were down, so she wondered if it jumped through one. Watching as they drove away to see if she saw it, she never did.

As it turns out, the woman, at the time, was wearing a long black skirt. We wonder if the cat was Minnie and thought she had found her owner. This would be why she followed the couple and jumped on the woman's lap. Perhaps, once she realized it wasn't her owner, she decided to jump out and go back to Hebron Cemetery to wait for her. Maybe, Minnie is bound to the cemetery and cannot leave, and that's why she exited the vehicle as it passed through the exit. Of course, it could have been just a stray cat. As anyone who has spent any significant time around cats knows, they can move in some very erratic ways.

WALT STILL AT DISNEY
(from *Be Our Ghost*)

We explored the reports that Walt Disney still haunts Disneyland in our previous book, *Haunts of Hollywood Stars and Starlets,* in which we also discussed Disney's rise to fame. Undoubtedly, Walt Disney is one of the most important names in the entertainment world. The Chicago native persevered through many failures and misfortunes to build one of the biggest media empires the world has ever known. He has won twenty-six Academy Awards and is one of the greatest pioneers in animation. His parks attract millions of people around the world each year. Now, with the recent acquisitions of Lucasfilm, Marvel Studios, 20th Century Fox, and Fox Searchlight, the Walt Disney Company seems unstoppable.

The same goes for Walt himself. Despite his death, nothing seems to be able to stop him from visiting his beloved park. There are reports that he haunts a few different areas around Disneyland.

Walt had an apartment above the fire station on Main Street, U.S.A. in Disneyland. Whenever he stayed there, he kept a light burning in the window to let workers know he was there. After his death, the staff wished to leave the room just as Walt had, with only minimal tidying. Rumor has it the apartment is almost exactly how it was when Walt passed, with even his workpapers still lying on his desk as they were. We're not sure if that part of the story is true however, because when researching the apartment, we found that it has been restored to the exact state it was in when the park first opened in 1955, and that tours of the apartment are available. We have not seen the apartment for ourselves, so we are not sure which version of the story is true.

However, there is a story about a cleaning lady who had an encounter with the ghost of Walt Disney. Not long after he died, the cleaning lady was touching up the room and when she finished, she turned off the light in the window. When she got back outside, she looked up and saw that the light shining in the window. Thinking maybe she had neglected to turn it off all the way, she went back in and made sure to extinguish it completely. Again, when she got back out to the street, she saw someone had relit the lamp.

Now concerned that someone was in there, she went back in and looked around, finding no one present. She then turned the light off again and stayed in the room to see if it came back on. A few seconds later, it did. Then she heard a voice whisper, "I'm still here." She left the apartment and never went back inside. Now, people supposedly only enter the apartment to relight the lamp when it burns out.

There is one version of the story we reported in *Haunts of Hollywood* that claims the cleaning lady unplugged the lamp, but it came back on, and she then saw someone pull back the curtains in the room and look out at her. While it's very possible the curtain part of this story is true, we doubt seriously she pulled the plug on the lamp since the lamp is not electric. We have never been to Disneyland to see the lamp for ourselves, and we have just learned this recently. Misinformation is sometimes the issue when reporting urban legends and ghost tales, and we usually go the extra mile to ensure we have the story right. Unfortunately, this was an oversight on our end.

Employees who entered the room to relight the lamp have heard loud knocks on the walls and footsteps moving across the room. Some who have been down in the firehouse below have reported hearing bangs, knocks, and footsteps coming from the apartment above them.

A well-respected psychic medium named Michael Kouri released a book called *The Ghost of Walt Disney & Me* chronicling his time spent in the apartment with the likes of Roy Disney and author Ray Bradbury. While there, Kouri reported strange and frightening occurrences began, such as the toilet flushing, faucets running, strange sounds in the cupboards, and even phantom phone calls with nothing more than static on the other end.

In 2009, a Disneyland security camera caught the transparent image of a man walking from the Haunted Mansion and through the park after hours. He walked through fences and across water. Since the video surfaced on YouTube, it has led to many debates about the nature of the image. Some say it's an image from old footage bleeding over, but others seem to think it's the ghost of Walt Disney taking a stroll through his beloved park. Those who believe it's a ghost ask why it was only one man's image burned into the footage. They also ask why he was moving so quickly through the park. These are both interesting questions to consider. Personally, we think it's odd that the person's entire walk was visible. Was the image metaphysical or just a simple malfunction in technology?

The area above the Pirates of the Caribbean ride in Disneyland allegedly houses the spirit of Walt, as well as his wife Lillian. At one time, this was the Disney Gallery, an exhibition of artwork from Walt Disney Imagineering. For twenty years, from 1987 to 2007, it was in the area above POTC in New Orleans Square. The Gallery has since moved, but during the two decades it was there, people reported seeing Walt and Lillian Disney walking around the Formal Sitting Room, enjoying the artwork. They were also seen in the Collector's Room, sitting down as if relaxing after a long day. Walt often stood in the vestibule by himself, as if waiting for Lillian. Lillian lingered on the balcony and patio after close.

Some believe Walt likes to watch the firework display brighten the night sky over Sleeping Beauty Castle. There is a forty-second video on YouTube that shows the end of the show, and some think this video captured the image of Walt Disney's ghost standing on the castle, looking up at the fireworks. If you look closely at the image in the video, you can see that it is most certainly the image of a person. It's not smoke making the shape of a human as it remains in place, not drifting as smoke does. It looks like a back shot of the Partners statue, where Walt is holding Mickey Mouse's hand and pointing. There is a Partners in Disney World and in front of Sleeping Beauty Castle, but there is no such statue *on* Sleeping Beauty Castle. What's more, once the firework show ends, the figure looks as if it turns around and begins walking, only to fade away.

It is an interesting video. We watched several more videos and looked at many pictures of the Disneyland firework show and never saw the image again. Now, could it have been some holographic image of Walt? Maybe so. Disney likes to slide in hidden gems like that into their shows, movies, and attractions. Only it seems there would be other videos with the shot in them.

This reminds us of a story we read while researching Walt's apartment on Main Street. On Disneyland's opening day, the Mouseketeers were in Walt's apartment with him watching everyone enter. One Mouseketeer said that when all the people came pouring in, Walt stood there with his hands behind his back, tears in his eyes, and a grin on his face. The mysterious image on top of Sleeping Beauty Castle is reminiscent of that description.

We can't say if that shape captured on video was truly the ghost of Walt Disney, or a ghost at all, but it certainly is interesting to view. Perhaps he is still standing in Disneyland, watching the wonders that have come out of it since his death, still smiling at the colossal achievement. If it's true that Walt's spirit remains at Disneyland, we're also glad to hear Lillian is with him. Nothing better than sharing eternity with your dream and the person you loved most in the world.

OPEN THIS DOOR, YOU DEAD PEOPLE!

(from *Jenny is the Strange and Unusual*)

The inspiration to create our own ghost tour came from three separate individuals who had their own paranormal tours. One was in Bardstown, KY; another in Downtown Louisville; and the other was in Old Louisville.

At first, when we attended those tours, we had no intention of starting tours of our own. However, after having gone on them, and hearing all the ghost stories in Shepherdsville and "NuLu," we thought of how much fun we'd had on those two tours and that we would like to do something similar, bringing that kind of enjoyment to others while sharing the stories in person.

We were already involved in ghost hunting, now learning from experience as much as from research, and we both knew we could do it. So, we did, but in between that, we returned to a few of the locations on the other hosts' tours to investigate on our own. So, we visited several locations throughout those tours, even going as far to stay overnight at the Seelbach Hotel, the Old Talbott Tavern, and the Jailer's Inn.

Our style of investigation isn't as, what some would call "scientific," as others. We didn't have enough equipment to film our own movies like some hunters do. That's not to say we don't think that's cool or see the merit in that approach. The more avenues of exploration you use, the better your chances of capturing any evidence. Jacob always said I was equipment enough, as I seem to sense the spirits, and they sense me. So, our primary piece of equipment was the spirit box. Jacob would bring his cameras and, sometimes, a digital recorder; he also brought his laptop along a few times. There were a few times I took some dowsing rods with me, and sometimes a trigger object, if the paranormal reports at the location provided the right environment for it. Mostly, it was the box.

Some people who didn't believe our approach "right" or "real ghost hunting" called us the "Ghost Box Kids," in a derisive manner. I suspect, as does Jacob, they did this because of the interesting responses and pictures we often captured, and the attention that evidence would get on our pages, as a way to try to dismiss them.

Though you'll find many welcoming people in the paranormal community—particularly among those who take the more sensitive approach, like empaths and psychics and other true believers—sadly, there are many who act as if the entire endeavor is a constant competition of one-upmanship consisting of not only obtaining "better" evidence, but also attacking and trying to discredit someone else's evidence, even if their evidence is, ultimately, no different.

Some seemed to have the idea of making you "kiss the ring" or "pay your dues" by serving their groups. There are no dues to pay in the paranormal community. You either have the gift, or you don't; you either know how to use the gift, or you don't; you either capture evidence, or you don't. There are no guidelines, no hierarchy. Unfortunately, many seem to think that's how it works, and it doesn't. Due to this, we quickly learned to avoid groups and organizations and go our own way, which worked out much better for us.

A funny side note: The individual who mockingly dubbed us the "Ghost Box Kids" was known for posting pictures of dust and calling them orbs, and saying cigarette smoke in pictures were spirits. At the beginning of the investigation at the poor farm, he showed a picture he took to Jacob, claiming the blurry image he captured was a ghost. Immediately, Jacob said, "That looks like a finger on the lens." The guy insisted it wasn't, but it clearly was. People who had worked with him before later told us that he tries to pass off mundane things as paranormal evidence and even goes as far as faking photos. I don't know if that's true, because, as I just previously stated, people say that a lot about others in the community, but he certainly revealed his own personality as not being too welcoming, and treating this as a competition, so maybe there's some merit to this information.

During our visits to the Old Talbott Tavern and the Jailer's Inn, we didn't capture anything we felt was very revealing. We did receive some intelligent responses at the poor farm in Indiana, where I first investigated with my former co-worker. There was much activity at the Seelbach Hotel, which we originally wrote about in *Louisville's Strange and Unusual Haunts*, then added to the more recent, and more extensive, *Kentucky's Strange and Unusual Haunts*.

There was a funny incident that happened when we were investigating the poor farm. As we were sitting around in a room, trying to speak to the spirits, the room suddenly began to shake. This, of course, surprised us all. The coworker, who was a former fulltime ghost hunter, tried to come up with a scientific explanation. I don't recall what she decided. After a few minutes, we eventually figured out, after hearing the whistle, that it was a train passing. We had not been aware of the railroad track only a few yards from the building prior to that.

I mentioned the Bullitt County History and Genealogical Society allowing us to investigate the Old Stone Jail, and how helpful some of the individuals—particularly David Strange—were. When investigated, it was at night, after the history museum's business hours, and they unlocked the jail for us. When setting up the laptop inside, Jacob saw a shadow moving outside the window at the back of the jail, which is situated in something of a cul-de-sac nestled in a corner of the second Bullitt County Courthouse. The courthouse surrounded the jail on three sides by the courthouse walls, with plenty of space between the front door and the steps on one side, but the other two creating relatively narrow alleys. It was in one of these alleys he saw the shadow moving beyond the window when no one was out there.

I also experienced a shadow person inside the jail, near one of the cells. Inside that cell, something pinched me on the backside during a spirit box session, with a scratch following. The scratch wasn't horrific, but it did leave a mark.

While waiting for guests to arrive, one patron told us she also received a scratch inside that jail—in the same cell! The way she described it, her scratch was much deeper, and longer, leaving quite the wound on her left ankle.

We do miss those tours, but it had to end due to Jacob's spinal and feet issues. I also live with some physical issues of my own, one being idiopathic intracranial hypertension, also known as pseudotumor cerbri, which causes spinal fluid to backup and swell, causing me a lot of neurological issues. The ninety-minutes or more spent walking and standing on our feet became too much. We have considered finding a way to relaunch the Shepherdsville tour, so maybe one day.

The Shepherdsville tour was a fun tour for everyone. Our guests were so kind and welcomed it. They always seemed to have a good time and were fascinated with the town and the stories. Many came for ghosts but loved the history as we took them around the historic district to the sites. They often said it felt like they were going on adventure. Many times, guests revealed to us they never knew about these historic stories, or much about the town; some didn't even know about Shepherdsville at all, or had never been there. We ended up turning many people on to the history museum and Bullittcountyhistory.org. That was very satisfying for us, to bring attention to such an interesting little town.

The NuLu tour wasn't the adventure the Shepherdsville tour was, as it was just a straight shot down the street, with all stops but one being on the same side of East Market Street. The ghost stories were more detailed, with some even connecting. What made that tour special was Joe Ley's Antiques was the first stop, and my mother worked there for over twenty years.

The folks at Joe Ley's were happy to tell us the history, but weren't too excited about the reported haunts. Joe, being old fashioned, feared it would chase customers away. His daughter tried to explain to him that these days people are interested in the paranormal and the prospect of possible ghosts might draw people to the location. She even told us she was going to "make up a ghost just to get people in there," but she didn't need to do that. There were several ghost stories about that place.

One local author, who sent someone to interview us about some of the places we discovered during our research, ended up taking that information and writing about Joe Ley's in his own book about Louisville (we were not the only ones he did this to; he did it even worse to the man who spent years researching Old Louisville ghost stories and wrote several books about them; and he actually lived in the neighborhood during the time) In it, he included a note that the owner insists the place isn't haunted, despite some people saying it is.

Of course, with all books and both tours, we never claimed to corroborate the stories we heard. Those we experienced ourselves were obviously our accounts, and we would say so. What these experiences could have been we left for others to interpret. We simply told the stories others told us. We didn't even include the personal experiences I had in the building, nor what my mother experienced.

Other than that, everyone else down there in NuLu was very accepting and willing to help us. The Taj Bar, the Red Tree, the St. John's Church—all were very supportive. As for our book, Prophecy Ink, the tattoo and art gallery on Baxter Avenue, was also very welcoming as they told us of their ghost, Little Bastard.

The building was once a barber shop, and they had an old book with hair clippings and pictures of those the clippings belonged to, and they gave it to us. This is also where I got my first tattoo. If you're in or around Louisville, I highly recommend them. They are great people who do exceptional work and conduct business at the highest order of professionalism.

Diorio's Pizza right next door was very accommodating. The owner not only told us of the experiences people had (we also heard more afterwards from a couple other people), he also gave us a complete tour of the building, while telling us some of the history. There is an interesting door to nowhere there, and Muhammed Ali used to box in the upstairs area before he made it to the professional ranks.

The St. John's Church, which, at the time, had three locations—the church, the Parish House, and the Parish Hall (Jacob nicknamed this the St. John's Three; unfortunately, St. John's no longer owns the Parish Hall, and so it has no more connection to the church), was very welcoming. Not only did they share a lot of historical information, they were open to the paranormal, so much so that they told us many encounters, and even allowed us to host two public paranormal investigations there.

During the research, and the investigation, they granted us access to the bell tower, which is home to a creepy shadowy presence lurking on the stairs and staring down at those below. The church, as well as the other locations, were so interesting to others, we had someone come from New York to go on our tour.

A few news articles featured Jacob discussing the tour around that time. The word spread, and people were interested. When our book released, it did very well locally. Still, I have never quite taken it all in.

BETTIE PAGE
(from *Death and Lipstick*)

B ettie Page was an American model in the 1950s, known for her iconic pin-up photos, earning her the nickname the "Queen of Pinups."

Her jet-black hair, blue eyes, and trademark bangs have been an influential fashion statement for generations of artists. After her death, *Playboy* founder Hugh Hefner called her "a remarkable lady, an iconic figure in pop culture who influenced sexuality, taste in fashion; someone who had a tremendous impact on our society".

Born in Nashville, Tennessee, Page moved to California in her early adult years before moving to New York City in search of work as an actress. While in the Big Apple, she found work as a pin-up model, posing for several photographers throughout the fifties. Page was one of the first playmates for *Playboy*, being Miss January 1955.

In 1959, Page converted to evangelical Christianity and worked for Billy Graham, studying at Bible colleges in Los Angeles and Portland, Oregon. She intended to become a missionary. However, mental illness marked the latter part of Page's life, such as depression, violent mood swings, and several years in a state psychiatric hospital with paranoid schizophrenia.

At the height of her career, Bettie's mental health declined. She suffered episodes of psychosis often marked by violence and religious fanaticism.

In 1972, the police found her running through a motel complex waving a gun and threatening the retribution of God. A month later, she forced her ex-husband and his children to pray to a picture of Jesus at knifepoint, threatening to cut out their eyes and guts if they looked away. This led to a four-month hospitalization. It was during this stay when psychiatrists diagnosed her with paranoid schizophrenia.

Upon release, Bettie moved back in with her ex-husband to recover. Not long after she moved in, her ex had to call the police because she trashed his house in a fit of rage. Police detained Page, at which point she began to masturbate in the police car. This incident resulted in a six-month hospitalization for Bettie, where doctors placed her under a suicide watch.

In 1979, she attacked her elderly landlord with a knife. For this, she faced the charge of assault with a deadly weapon but was found not guilty by reason of insanity. She received a sentence of five years in a state hospital, but served less than a year.

Shortly after release, Bettie broke into the apartment of her new landlord, another elderly woman, and told her, "God has inspired me to kill you." Bettie stabbed the terrified woman repeatedly. The result was gruesome as Bettie sliced the woman from the corner of her mouth to her ear, severed a finger, and stabbed her four times in the chest. In defense of herself, the woman ended up with many wounds on her hands. Thankfully, she survived.

Bettie pled not guilty by reason of insanity and was sentenced to confinement in a state mental hospital for eight-and-a-half years and served the entirety of her sentence.

Bettie Page suffered greatly from a severe case of mental illness. While her crimes were both heinous and dangerous, before passing judgement, one should consider the state of mind she was in during those times. Clearly, she needed help, and by releasing her early, the system did her no favors and put others at risk. Mental healthcare is not a luxury for people who want to feel good. It is a necessary part of a civilized society.

Queen of Pin-Ups
Bettie Mae Page
Apr. 22, 1923 | Dec. 11, 2008

THE HAUNTED HILLTOP: KENTUCKY'S CREEPIEST COLLEGE CAMPUS

———◉———

(from *Kentucky's Strange and Unusual Haunts*)

In 1876, A.W. Mell founded the privately owned Glasgow Normal School and Business College in Glasgow, Kentucky. In 1884, the facility moved to Bowling Green, which received its first bit of land in 1797, and became the Southern Normal School and Business College, owned by Henry Hardin Cherry. When the Kentucky General Assembly approved legislation for two more teacher training facilities, Cherry sold the school to the state, and Western Kentucky State Normal School was born.

The school, no longer privately owned, came under control of the state with Cherry as the facility's first president. The normal school operated at that location until February of 1911 when it moved to its present-day location on College Heights, also known as the Hill, where the Pleasant J. Potter College once stood. The Hill stands 125 feet above the city, overlooking downtown Bowling Green. In 1922, it was renamed Western Kentucky State Normal School and Teachers College and began programs for four-year degrees.

After merging with a private men's college, known as Ogden College, in 1927, the institution became known as the Western Kentucky State Teachers College in 1930. As the mission of the school changed over the years, it underwent another name change in 1948, becoming Western Kentucky State College. Throughout the late 50s and early 60s, major expansion and restructuring took place at the college. In June of 1963, it merged with the Bowling Green College of Commerce, which could run as a separate institution. Three other colleges formed as part of Western's ever-growing campus in 1965: The Potter College of Liberal Arts; the Ogden College of Science and Technology; and the College of

Education. The name of the school changed the following year to Western Kentucky University and has continued to grow, becoming the state's third largest public college behind the University of Kentucky and the University of Louisville.

Though WKU might only be the third largest college, it seems to be the most haunted. Staff and students alike have told many tales of paranormal activity, ghostly encounters, and unexplained phenomena. The university embraces the paranormal claims and is not shy about sharing them. Among the locations said to haunted at WKU are Barnes-Campbell Hall, Florence Schneider Hall, the Academic Complex, Greek Houses, McLean Houses, the Kentucky Museum, the Margie Helm Library, Pearce-Ford Tower, Potter Hall, Rodes-Harlin Hall, Sigma Alpha Epsilon House, Lambda Chi Alpha Fraternity, and Van Meter Hall. A plethora of articles and books about the alleged hauntings exist, and we dug through quite a bit to gather the information.

Let's begin, shall we?

VAN METER HALL

The current Van Meter Hall sits at the top of the Hill and is one of campus's original buildings. Built in 1911, it replaced the old Vanmeter Hall, built in 1901 as a replacement to the main building of the Southern Normal School & Business College which burned to the ground in 1900. The second and current building, which is on the National Registry of Historic Places, has a haunted auditorium.

The namesake for the building is Capt. Charles J. Vanmeter, one of Bowling Green's most respected and generous philanthropists, as well as one of the town's oldest natives upon his death in 1913 at the age of 86. It was he who provided the funds for the building of the original Vanmeter Hall.

The Van Meter Auditorium is for theater, but there have been concerts and presentations held there as well. There are three different stories about the ghost that allegedly haunts there. The most accepted account is that during construction a worker was on the roof and fell through the skylight to the lobby floor, dying on impact. A plane flying overhead supposedly distracted the man, which might have been a fascinating sight to folks in those days. The man's body left behind a large puddle of blood that doesn't seem to go away. Supposedly, whenever someone washes the floor, the stain returns. Allegedly, the bloodstain glows during events. During these events, his ghost is known to appear in front of students and staff, scaring them. He also likes to cause a little mischief in the auditorium by opening and closing the stage curtain, turning the lights on and off, causing inexplicable computer malfunctions, and moving tables and music stands around the building. The man's wife and child haunt the auditorium, wandering about, singing, and talking unintelligibly.

Another version of the tale is that a member of the custodial staff was hanging lights above the stage and fell to the floor and left the unrelenting bloodstain. No matter how many times someone washes the spot where he landed, the stain always returned. Eventually, the auditorium required a new floor because of this. Whether it is the construction worker or custodian, people have reported seeing a phantom sitting in a seat in one of the back rows when the auditorium was otherwise empty.

The least-known story is the most interesting. In this tale, there are supposed to be caverns under Van Meter Hall where a hermit once dwelt. This hermit carried a blue lantern with him through the dark passages, and after he died in the tunnels below his spirit found a path that leads into Van Meter Hall and now wanders in the shadows carrying a blue lantern that resembles one of those blue light police cameras seen hanging off streetlights.

POTTER HALL

One of the oldest buildings on the campus, Potter Hall, built in 1921 and named after J. Whit Potter, who was president of Potter-Matlock Trust Company and the American National Bank, and was also a regent of Western Kentucky State Normal School. The three-story residence hall was originally a women's dormitory that had a monthly rent of $8.50. During World War II, from 1942 till the end of 1943, Army Air Corps cadets stayed there. In 1949, Potter's Hall became a men's dorm until 1957, once again becoming a woman's dorm due to the building of two new men's dorms. As of 1994, Potter Hall has been an administration building consisting of a registrar, financial aid consulting, admissions, student counseling, and career services.

Potter Hall has a very dark and poignant legend attached to it. On April 21st, 1979, Theresa Watkins, nicknamed Tye-Dye, a student who lived in room seven on the ground floor, took a belt and hanged herself from some steam heating pipes running along the ceiling of her dorm room. Supposedly, there are funeral records documenting this, though we have not seen them ourselves. There are also a few reports of paranormal activity taking place in the building.

There have been two spirits to have allegedly identified themselves, neither of which call themselves Theresa, but go by the names of Casperella and Allison instead. On separate occasions, students using a Ouija board have communicated with both spirits. Casperella confided in those she chatted with that she was a very sad spirit that likes to bother residents there by locking and unlocking doors, rattling desk drawers, and making creepy noises up and down the halls. Allison claimed she likes to take people's items and move and even hide them.

These incidents allegedly described by these spirits via Ouija boards have been known to happen. Some ladies who used to live there reported hearing footsteps in the hall, followed by their name being softly spoken just outside their door. Whenever they answered the voice or gone to check the halls, no one was there.

Some residents and faculty members describe a feeling of unease in the basement storage room where Watkins hanged herself. People report the usual cold spots, sense of dread, and feeling of someone watching. Others say her ghost often bangs on the pipe from which she hung, but this could very well be normal plumbing issues.

Many believe that both spirits are Theresa going by a different name. We think maybe the students gave the spirit the name of Casperella, and they probably didn't receive a name from her. Allison, though, was reportedly the name given during the other Ouija board session. Perhaps Theresa has her reasons for not wanting her true name known.

Since it has become an office building, there is a spirit that moves from room to room stealing pennies, leaving them lying around the building, and rolling them down the hall. No one knows why it does this, but because of this, people call the ghost Penny. Some faculty members have reported seeing pennies carried away by the spirits. One staff member in the building reported hearing coins dropping into a vending machine when no one was out around the machines. We're not sure if this is Theresa Watkins, but Penny sure carries the tell-tale trait of mischievousness that comes with the paranormal accounts coming from Potter Hall.

FLORENCE SCHNEIDER HALL

This three-story Georgian Revival building was constructed in 1929, originally called West Hall due to its location on the Hill's western slope. A few years later it would be renamed Whitestone Hall. It was an all-women's dormitory built to house 200 young ladies. The second floor had a large room used for conferences, studies, and other general uses. On the third floor was the infirmary, complete with metal hospital furniture, a diet kitchen, and the nurses' living quarters. Just as with Potter Hall, Army Air Corps cadets stayed there during World War II.

The building became a continuing education center in 1977. This was short lived as it soon became an all-women's dorm again in 1980 due to a housing shortage. But over the next few years, enrollment of female students severely declined, leading to the closing of the hall in 1984. It was then rented out as office space and conference rooms until the first two floors became co-ed dorms in 1987. As of 2007, Florence Schneider Hall houses the Gatton Academy of Mathematics and Science in Kentucky.

Schneider Hall has quite a distinctive history. But there is something far more sinister tied to its past.

There's a campus legend that sometime during Spring Break in the late 1940s, when the building was known as Whitestone Hall, two students had stayed behind to complete a project for one of their classes. During the night, an escaped lunatic wielding an ax dragged himself up the fire escape and entered through a window on one of the upper floors. He then found the stairways and took them to the floor below. From there, he slipped into a room at the end of the hall and attacked one of the students, whose name was Judy.

The story says that Judy was studying at her desk at the time, though we don't know how that can be known for sure under the circumstances. In any event, she saw the killer and screamed, prompting him to strike her with the ax and apparently flee the scene. Severely wounded and heavily bleeding, the young lady dragged herself into the hall and scratched at the other student's door. Having heard the commotion, the other woman was too terrified to answer. The next morning, when she stepped out into the hall, she found Judy's body with the ax embedded into her head.

Though there is no documentation of this alleged murder, some residents at Schneider Hall believe it could explain the strange and spooky things they have seen over the years. Women have found themselves locked in the bathrooms despite leaving the doors unlocked when they went in. Doors slam shut mysteriously up and down the halls. Many students have reported hearing disembodied footsteps moving through rooms and down hallways.

Some have seen Judy sitting at windows inside, as well as standing in doorways. Others have claimed to see a pale apparition looking at them from windows while they were outside. Some say the image of a ghostly woman wanders through rooms. It appears that Judy has an affinity for electrical gadgets, such as televisions, computers, lamps, and alarm clocks, as she often turns them on and off. People blame her for the chairs, beds, and tables that sometimes move on their own.

The occurrence that seems to chill residents the most happens during Spring Break. The sound of scratching on doors in the middle of the night have terrified some of the students who stayed behind. Many believe that this is Judy trying to make her presence known, perhaps believing she is still on the run from an ax-wielding homicidal maniac.

THE HELMS LIBRARY

Originally known as the Health & Physical Education Building, WKU had the Helms Library built in 1931 for about $250,000. Initially, it was a gymnasium referred to as the Big Red Barn. After the construction of Diddle Arena in 1963, the building became a library, dedicated on October 14th, 1967.

The namesake for the library was Auburn, KY native Margie Helms. Helms was a well-educated woman who became WKU's librarian assistant in 1920, then the librarian in 1923, and finally the Director of Library Services in 1956, which she served as until her retirement in 1965. In 1950, she received the Outstanding Business Woman of Bowling Green Award from the Business and Professional Woman's Club. The Kentucky Library Association presented her with the Outstanding College Librarian for Kentucky Award in 1964.

As rumor has it, there was a student many years ago who was up on the ninth floor of the building and decided to open the window but had some difficulty because it was stuck. After wrestling with the window, it popped open. The force pulled the student forward, and seeing as there was no screen, he fell through the opening and plummeted to his death. Now, his spirit haunts the ninth floor. People have seen him standing near the window and walking the halls. Some have reported hearing the echo of his final scream as he tumbles through the open window. Some say the window will open on its own. At night, or while alone on the floor, someone will find the window open, shut it, and find it open again soon after. Many think the boy's ghost is behind this action.

THE KENTUCKY MUSEUM

When history teacher Gabriella Robertson noticed there was only one book on Kentucky in the library of the Western Kentucky State Normal School in 1914, she set out to change that. She eventually succeeded in amassing enough books on Kentucky history to warrant the requesting of a new building in which to store them. President Dr. Cherry agreed and decided that he not only wanted the library, but a museum, and he began to raise money for it through the College Heights Foundation in 1928. After he raised the money, construction of the Kentucky Building began in 1931 and completed on November 16th, 1939, which was also Cherry's birthday.

The building held the library and museum, as well as classrooms and reception areas. of the school stored several artifacts, such as family bibles, letters from GIs to their girlfriends, children's toys, photographs, furniture, clothing, jewelry, and other items in the building. The building closed in 1976 but reopened in 1980 after undergoing some major renovations.

Many people have reported strange and frightening occurrences in the Kentucky Building. These reports have led to the belief that the building is haunted, particularly in the museum. Some faculty members have seen dark shapes moving in their periphery, only to turn and see no one near. Shadow figures move in corners and across rooms. Dark silhouettes linger in doorways and stand in the halls near the museum. After spotting these forms, visitors will leave the room and hear rapid footsteps trailing them. Many who have seen these figures claim sudden gusts of freezing cold air accompany them. Usually, witnesses feel the eerie sensation of someone watching them before they see the figures.

Though the museum holds the most chilling haunt in the building, the library has its own ghosts as well. Books have jumped from shelves and tables directly onto the floor by an unseen force. Some believe this to be the ghost of a young man whose apparition was filmed walking through the museum. Several witnesses have spotted this young man passing through the library and they believe it to be the spirit of a former student.

MCLEAN HALL

Designed by John Wilson and Maurice Ingram, McLean Hall was built in 1947 for a cost of a half-million dollars. At the time, it was one of two female dorms on campus, the other being the Florence Schneider Hall, then known as Whitestone Hall. It housed 160 female students across 90 rooms. Other than the resident rooms, it also had laundry facilities, a social room, and a reception area.

Its namesake, Miss Mattie McLean, graduated from the State Normal School in 1902 and became secretary to then-Western president, Dr. Henry Hardin Cherry. When Cherry died in 1937, she served under the next president, Paul Garrett. She also served on the Board of Regents as well. In 1945, after forty-three years of service to the university, Miss McLean retired and moved to Mississippi, where she lived the rest of her life, passing away from a stroke on December 8th, 1954.

McLean Hall was quiet of any paranormal activity for many years until three students decided to pick up a Ouija board one night and see if they could contact her. Disembodied footsteps walking the halls at night compelled them to do this, as well as the sounds of someone entering rooms. This led the ladies to believe that this was perhaps Miss Mattie McLean walking the halls and checking on the rooms, perhaps keeping watch over the young women staying in the hall.

According to the legend, they asked if Miss Mattie was in the room, to which the spirit replied, "Yes." They then asked her if she would be willing to materialize so they could see her, and the spirit again replied, "Yes." Next, the young ladies claimed they turned off the lights, and a light began to glow before them. In seconds, a gray-haired woman with a gray face and wearing a gray outfit appeared. From there, they say they asked the entity questions about Miss Mattie's life, and when they researched the answers later, they found that the ghost had answered them correctly.

There is a portrait of Mattie McLean hanging in McLean Hall. Since this incident, the light beneath it will turn on and off by itself and even glow brighter sometimes. Other reports claim that if you stare long enough at it, the image of Miss Mattie will smile at you. Maybe she feels welcome since talking to these students and wants to let them know she continues to watch over them.

BARNES-CAMPBELL HALL

Located on the south end of the campus, this nine-story men's residence hall went up in 1966 and named after Sheridan Barnes and Donald Campbell, two Board of Regents members in the 1950s.

During spring break about a year after the building's construction, a 20-year-old RA out of Leitchfield named James Wilbur Duvall stepped out of the shower and noticed that the elevator car was stuck between the 6th and 7th floors. This was apparently a regular occurrence, and Duvall had fixed this issue a few times before. So, instead of walking up the stairs, he opened the door to the shaft with an elevator key with the intention of flipping the switch that would get the car moving again. Only he did not ensure that the elevator car was not descending upon him. When he leaned into the shaft and reached for the switch, the car pinned him between the outer wall of the shaft and a steal beam, crushing him to death. Since this tragedy, rumor has it his spirit still haunts the halls.

According to several eyewitness reports, sometimes, late in the evening, when the elevator stops on the fifth floor, the doors will open to reveal no passengers inside. Some have even reported a rush of cold air emitting from the empty car. Others who have rode the elevator say it will stop on the fifth floor even though no one has pressed the button. The elevator will also ride up and down with no one inside, sometimes late at night. Many believe this to be Duvall's spirit riding the elevator to his floor.

During spring break, after all the students were gone, a faculty member had just finished sweeping Barnes-Campbell Hall to ensure no students were there. After finding all residents were gone, he went out for dinner. Upon returning to retrieve something from the fifth floor RA's room, he found all the water faucets and showers turned on, along with a trail of wet footprints leading from the bathroom to the RA's room while no one else was in the building.

This isn't the only incident of mysterious bathroom activity, however. Students have reported hearing the showers running late at night when everyone was supposed to be asleep. When investigating the sounds, they found the bathroom empty with the water running. Others have even seen the wet footprints leading from the bathroom to the elevator.

This spirit doesn't confine itself to the bathroom, elevator, and RA room only. People entered rooms in the morning and found chairs moved around. Some chairs have slammed against the walls, thrown by unseen forces. Many attribute this activity to the ghost of James Wilbur Duvall.

There definitely seems to be some strange occurrences taking place in the Barnes-Campbell Hall. With such a tragedy having taken place, it seems the spirit of Mr. Duvall may still be lingering.

RODES-HARLIN HALL

Also known as Dormitory No. 4, WKU added Rodes-Harlin Hall in 1966 and named after John B. Rodes and Max B. Harlin. Rodes was a close friend of WKU president, Dr. Cherry, and a former Mayor of Bowling Green from 1929 to 1933 and Warren Circuit Judge in 1948. Harlin was a Tennessee native who moved to Bowling Green in 1909 to open a law practice and served as a WKU regent from 1928 to 1932.

Rodes-Harlin Hall is nine stories and houses up to 400 female students. Allegedly, a former student there chose to take her life by jumping from the roof of the building. Not long after her death, students who knew her would hear tapping and scratching on their windows, even those on the upper floors. When they looked out to see what was causing it, only the dark, empty night was there to greet them. These reports lessened as the students living in the building when she died graduated and moved on, but even today the occasional student reports these mysterious sounds just outside their windows where there is nothing to make them.

But, the young woman's spirit did not cease her haunting. Some students and faculty believe she returns on the anniversary of her death to scare other students. She roams the halls of the ninth floor at night, tapping on doors. Whenever a curious student will step out into the hall to answer the knocks or investigate the footsteps, the woman will appear as a pale apparition in front of them.

On that night, she will also appear upon the roof to relive her final moments of life, and throw herself off, disappearing as she falls. Many believe this to be the source of the unexplained footsteps along the roof sometimes heard.

Is she there only on the anniversary of her death, or is that just when her presence is strongest?

THE GREEK HOUSES

Known for turning boys into men, with the mission to make each member into the best version of themselves they can possibly be, the fraternities of Western Kentucky University have their own collection of creeps and specters. Steeped in urban legends and unexplained occurrences, the tales from these houses are quite interesting.

The Phi Delta Theta fraternity has been around since 1848. It came to Western Kentucky on May 6th, 1966, led by a man named Bill Hatter. Today, there are over 100 members, ranging across many WKU organizations. Not without a sense of charity, Phi Delta Theta recently received the Clark Jackson Award for raising $17,000 between 2015 and 2016 for Lou Gehrig's disease and the ALS Association.

The house on Alumni Avenue has a history of suspected paranormal activity. An incessant and disturbing rattling of pipes and strange groans heard in the walls have led many to believe there is a menacing supernatural force in the house. Many attribute this to very mundane plumbing problems, though no plumbers have confirmed this, leading others to insist that ghosts haunt the walls.

A more peculiar tale is that of the moving stair rails. The age-worn staircase banister of the house is missing several rails, and it seems the rails that remain mysteriously switch places. House members have reported rails from the bottom moving to the top, and vice versa. Where there will be one missing rail in an area one day, there will be two missing there on another day, only to later see one of the rails returned to its spot. Sometimes, when a rail in one section has magically reappeared, another rail goes missing in another section. A spot that was previously missing a rail will suddenly have one in its place, only to see the rail move to an entirely different area of the banister. This has been a very perplexing occurrence to some members of the house.

The Delta Tau Delta house on Chestnut Street has a more specific haunt. It seems a former member of the house is still hanging around, letting people know he is there.

The origin of this once rebellious fraternity dates back to 1858 at Bethany College in West Virginia. When those who headed an organization of poets, orators, and essayists known as the Neotrophian Literary Society fixed a prize vote, eight angry men decided to form a secret society to combat this nepotistic society. Their goal was to take back control of this organization and return it to the student body. This organization became Delta Tau Delta, and it now has more than 170,000 members across 200 campuses nationwide.

They came to WKU in February 1967. WKU suspended their charter from the campus on July 22nd, 2014 due to a poor academic performance and low number of members. They returned in the fall of 2018 – ghost and all.

There is a room in the house members refer to as "Billy's Room." In the 1980s, a Delt by the name of Billy Lester died mysteriously in his room, and members believe his spirit remains there. The door to the room will suddenly open and slam shut when no one is in there. Lights turn on and off, and the stereo will often come on by itself, and the volume will go up full blast. Some students believe Billy is still there in his old room, perhaps trying to get other members' attention or simply unaware he has passed away.

Warren Albert Cole founded Lambda Chi Alpha in the early 1900s. There are two different accounts as to how this fraternity's formation came about. One recounts that in November of 1909, Cole met with Clyde Nichols and Percival Morse in Boston and pledged an allegiance to this new brotherhood. This meeting was intended to reorganize a society of law students from Boston University called the Cosmopolitan Law Club, but resulted in the Lambda Chi Alpha organization. The laws of this new fraternity are \ a mergence of the rites and regulations of a prep school fraternity known as Alpha Mu Chi, of which all men had been members, as well as a legal fraternity known as Gamma Eta Gamma and an agriculturist society known as the National Grange of the Order of Patrons of Husbandry, both of which Cole was a member.

The other story of Lambda Chi Alpha's creation states that when Cole first came to Boston University in 1909, his residence was very far from his law school. He and a few other students began renting a room at Pemberton Square where they could study between classes and work. Over time, this circle became known as the Tombs or Cosmopolitan Club. By the end of the year, he decided to move to a place on Joy Street. It was here that he shared an apartment with Charles Proctor and James McDonald who eventually joined Sigma Alpha Epsilon. Cole, however, wanted to start his own fraternity. Two years later, he moved to Hancock Street and roomed with Ralph Miles and Harold Bridge. On November 15th, along with Percival Morse, these men became the founders of Lambda Chi Alpha, basing their constitution largely on that of Gamma Eta Gamma's.

Lambda Chi Alpha came to Western Kentucky in 1965, housed in a building on Chestnut Street. Legend states that long before Lambda Chi Alpha moved in, the brutal murder of a young woman took place in that house. The story does not say who she was, but she is still there.

Past members have claimed to see the apparition of a young woman running across the lawn in distress. Whenever anyone approaches her, she disappears right in front of them. Other accounts describe the spirit chasing young men through the yard. Does she mistake them for her killer and try to chase them away, or are the unsuspecting students simply standing in her path as she dashes across the yard?

The young lady also seems to have an affinity for fire. One member of the Lambda Chi Alpha fell asleep with a candle burning on his nightstand only to wake and find the candle at the foot of his bed. Fireplaces in the building have lit on their own. Maybe it isn't that she's attracted to fire, but simply trying to get some light because she likes to turn lights on in the house. A chandelier inexplicably turns on by itself sometimes.

Kappa Sigma is a fraternity that has origins dating back as far as 1400 when a teacher at the University of Bologna in Italy named Manuel Chrysoloras took his five best disciples and formed a secret society for protection from the city's corrupt governor, pirate Baldassare Cossa (also known as Antipope John XXIII), who often had university students beaten and robbed in the streets. The society members used secret signals and codes to protect themselves from infiltrators. Over the centuries the society grew into something more than just a protective organization, it became a brotherhood. In 1869, five students at the University of Virginia took the traditions of the Bologna order and created Kappa Sigma to carry on its legacy.

Kappa Sigma came to WKU in 1965, and their house on College Street is allegedly haunted. A group of young men who were members of Kappa Sigma were experiencing strange occurrences in the house: loud unexplained noises, doors slamming shut, disembodied footsteps, and lights turning on and off. So, they decided to get a Ouija board to see who was causing these disturbances. According to their account, they contacted a spirit that called itself Jim the Cowboy who laid claim to the eerie happenings in the house. There isn't any information on who Jim the Cowboy is, but some insist that he is there.

The Sigma Alpha Epsilon house once found on College Street may have the most notorious spirits among the WKU fraternities. SAE began on March 9th, 1856, founded by eight men at the University of Alabama in Tuscaloosa. The leader was Noble Leslie DeVotie, who chose the name, wrote the ritual, and created the grip. It spread quickly across national campuses, coming to WKU on October 2nd, 1965.

The original building on College Street burned down in 2005, forcing the fraternity to move. The current house stands on the corner of Center Street and Alumni Avenue, and as far as we know, is clear of any spooks, creeps, or spirits. But the former house was allegedly a makeshift hospital during the Civil War. Former frat brothers who lived in the old house claimed they had seen some strange and spooky things: the faint image of a man appearing behind them in mirrors, and a humanly shadow that moves across walls when no one was walking by, with footsteps creaking along the floors as it passed. One evening, the ghost of a tall, skinny military man in an overcoat stood on the dance floor. After spotting this manifestation, they took out a Ouija board and tried to contact him. Upon doing so, the spirit confided that his name was Kevin and he had died in the hospital and was trapped in the house.

One peculiar comment Kevin made to them was that his favorite number is seven. It was in room seven that strange incidents occurred. The most chilling happened when a couple of fraternity members were in that room, and a refrigerator light suddenly went out, followed by the light in the room, and then the door slammed shut even though no one was standing near it.

During finals weeks, while the boys were in there studying, the answering machine kept activating. There were no messages left, but it kept switching on and beeping. One brother commented that he was glad there were no messages left at least, and the phone rang soon after. When someone answered the call, no one was on the other end.

In another room of the house, one student was getting frustrated with his roommate because he kept turning on a small fan they had sitting on a shelf. The student would get out of bed, turn the fan off, only to have it turned back on a few minutes later. After turning it off a couple more times, the next time the fan came back on, he got up to yell at his roommate but found he was alone in the room. As he stood there looking around, the fan flew from the shelf and hit the floor.

With lights burning out and fans turning on mysteriously, perhaps there were some major electrical issues taking place in the old building. If it was around during the Civil War, it no doubt had some wear and tear within its walls. Maybe that's why it eventually burned down. Investigators were quick to discover that the fire looked to be intentionally set. They determined that arson was the cause, not age. Luckily, there were only four students inside, and all woke in time thanks to the smoke detector, allowing them to escape unharmed. It's disappointing to think someone would set fire to a building with people inside, and as far as we know, authorities never caught the culprit. Perhaps it was Kevin trying to find a way out.

It's not just the boys who have ghosts in their Greek Houses. It seems the young ladies of the Kappa Delta sorority are not alone in their residence, as rumors of spectral encounters abound.

Four young students at the State Female Normal School in Farmville, Virginia founded Kappa Delta. On the rainy Saturday afternoon of October 23rd, 1897, Lenora Ashmore

Blackiston, Mary Sommerville Sparks Hendrick, Sara Turner White, and Julia Gardiner Tyler Wilson sat in their small dorm room in Professional Hall and developed Kappa Delta in hopes of empowering and inspiring young women to realize their full potential. Since then, this organization has grown to 250,000 women strong nationwide. The Delta Gamma chapter settled at Western Kentucky on March 27th, 1965.

The ghost of the woman by the name of Ms. Norman haunts there. Apparently, Ms. Norman was a widow who resided in the house long before the sorority, and allegedly built the house for her children and their families. Despite her intentions, her family rarely visited, and, saddled by the everlasting loneliness, hanged herself in the closet in what is now the house mom's room.

House moms in the past have heard strange rustling and thumps coming from that closet. Other members of the house have reported the sound of moans coming from the room as well as the basement. Footsteps walk along empty rooms and hallways in the night. The disembodied sounds of a woman crying have echoed softly through the house from an undetermined location.

THE ACADEMIC COMPLEX

This buildingon the southern end of the campus, built in 1969 and opened in 1970, is the home of the College of Health and Human Services, one of WKU's radio stations, and their TV broadcasting station, WKYU. The land used to be the location of Vets Village, where soldiers returning from war interested in education would stay in the 1940s and 50s. The building supposedly used to be a hospital at some point. The complex it seems, is haunted.

According to the stories, disc jockeys working there in the evening tend to have paranormal experiences. They have heard voices and footsteps coming from empty rooms. Some have reported seeing a human form moving around from the corner of their eye, only to turn and find no one there. Reportedly, there is a closet somewhere in the building that has a door that will swing wide and then slam shut randomly. On one occasion, two DJs there late into the night watched in shock as a CD player began moving on its own, as well as opening and closing.

PEARCE-FORD TOWER

At twenty-seven stories tall, Pearce-Ford Tower is the largest residence hall in the state of Kentucky. When it opened in 1970, it was the largest building in southern Kentucky, standing 247 feet. The name comes from William Pearce, who was director of WKU's Department of Extension and Correspondence from 1920 until 1959, and M.C. Ford who taught science and agriculture at WKU from 1913 until he passed away in 1940. Ford also served as the chair of Agricultural and Natural Sciences during his time at WKU.

The story behind the tower's alleged ghost is practically the same as the story from Barnes-Campbell Hall. A male student, who was supposedly one of the first to live there, didn't like to shower on his floor, so he went several floors up to use another shower. One evening, he went to the elevator to go back to his floor after showering, pushed the button and waited. When the doors opened, he stepped in without looking and plummeted twenty stories to his death, leaving only his wet footprints. The elevator, it seems, had become stuck on one of the floors above him.

Allegedly, on the anniversary of his death, the ghost of the young man relives his final moments. People have watched as his wet footprints appear on the floor, wandering from the shower to the elevator. Often, when the ghostly tracks halt at the elevator, the door will open with no one inside and then close.

Another story is that a worker fell to his death down the elevator shaft during the tower's construction. No one ever found his body, which may be entombed somewhere in the building, according to some. Some say when the building is closed for school breaks, faculty members checking the building have seen the elevator running up and down the shaft, stopping at random floors, while no one is inside.

We could not find any documentation to confirm these alleged deaths. However, it sounds like there is something going on with that elevator.

Well – pennies, and Ouija boards, and malfunctioning elevators; mysterious wet footprints, eerie voices in empty halls, and smiling portraits. Western Kentucky is a regular haven for haunting souls. While people often associate Kentucky's haunted locations with Waverly and Bobby Mackey's, it seems WKU outdoes them both in terms of alleged paranormal activity. There are many ghost stories emanating from this illustrious campus. Of course, some could be the result of over-imaginative young minds, while others could have been invented to scare underclassmen. But, aren't those the types of answers skeptics give about any place alleged to be haunted? There's no reason to believe that WKU's claims are any less authentic than the more infamous super-haunts.

Jenny is a paranormal investigator, author, psychic, thanatologist, tarot reader, and real-life Lydia Deetz who loves her crystals and haunts Shepherdsville, KY with her husband Jacob, three cats (Pandy, Bat-Bat, and Ariel), and many rabbits.

MORE NONFICTION FROM NIGHTMARE PRESS

KENTUCKY'S HAUNTED GRAVEYARDS

The Frightening Floyds

From The Frightening Floyds—authors of *Kentucky's Strange and Unusual Haunts*, *Aliens Over Kentucky*, and many other books on the mysterious and paranormal—comes *Kentucky's Haunted Graveyards*, a collection of spooky stories from various cemeteries across the Bluegrass State.

Within this book you will find abandoned cemeteries filled with spirits, celebrities' graves, a glowing tombstone, a haunted mausoleum, a sprawling necropolis filled with exquisite monuments, a woman in search of her black cat, a graveyard said to hold the Gates of Hell, and many more.

There are also some cemeteries not exactly haunted, but very strange and very unusual. Among them are a pet cemetery with a dark history, a haunting procession of lifelike statues, the bones of centuries-old martyrs displayed in a church, human bodies interred at a zoo, a family plot in a parking lot, and an airport and business compound built around a Native burial ground.

Join Jacob and Jenny Floyd as they bring you these creepy and weird stories in *Kentucky's Haunted Graveyards*.

JENNY'S SPOOKY LITTLE TALES: VOL. 2

The Frightening Floyds have been researching and writing about the paranormal and all things strange and unusual for ten years. To celebrate, Jenny recently compiled ten of her favorite stories from the many books she has written with her husband Jacob, which became *Jenny's Spooky Little Tales: Vol. 1*. Now, she has compiled ten more for *Jenny's Spooky Little Tales: Vol. 2*. In this collection, you'll find ghosts, a meat shower, a haunted Disney World attraction, spirits of Hollywood stars and starlets, the Bermuda Triangle, and even spooky tales from Louisville's famed Churchill Downs. We hope you enjoy *Jenny's Spooky Little Tales: Vol. 2*.

JENNY'S SPOOKY LITTLE TALES: VOL. 1

The Frightening Floyds have been researching and writing about the paranormal and all things strange and unusual for ten years. To celebrate, Jenny has compiled ten of her favorite stories from the many books she has written with her husband Jacob. In this collection, you'll find ghosts, aliens, a cursed Porsche, a forgotten graveyard, a family home, Disney haunts, and of course, Waverly Hills Sanatorium, among others. We hope you enjoy Jenny's Spooky Little Tales: Vol. 1.

JENNY IS THE STRANGE AND UNUSUAL

by Jenny Floyd

Thanatologist, ghost host, and paranormal author Jenny Floyd brings to you her journey from a small child seeing ghosts to an empath investigating the paranormal. Known as the Real-Life Lydia Deetz of Shepherdsville, she made her way into Louisville, establishing herself firmly in the paranormal community as an intuitive empath, also known as the Graveyard Girl.

Follow her life from the haunted homes in Shepherdsville, KY, to Joe Ley's Antiques in Louisville; from aspiring paranormal investigator to co-owner of two history and haunts tours; from researching ghosts to co-author of several books on the subject. You will see, herein, that Jenny's life truly has been strange and unusual.

DEATH AND LIPSTICK

by Jenny Floyd

Lipstick and a little bit of darkness combined with Old Hollywood, true crime, and ghost stories.

From the classic Lily Munster, celebrating her life in the shadows of a beloved Marilyn Monroe, to the tragedy of Carole Lombard, and Vampira's successful comeback; the sad and tragic murder of Sharon Tate to the not-so-glamorous side of Bettie Page, I want you to sit back, put on a cool pair of shades (and don't forget the lipstick) as I tell you about some of the scream queens and darkest divas from Hollywood's past and the makeup they loved.

KENTUCKY'S STRANGE AND UNUSUAL HAUNTS

by The Frightening Floyds

The Bluegrass State is home to many haunted legends. Stories of witches, ghosts, demons, monsters, "black things", "white thangs", and even headless horsemen abound across Kentucky. In this book you will read nearly a hundred of those legends taken from all across the state. From the hilltop of Western Kentucky University to the classy Seelbach Hotel, from the infamous Bobby Mackey's Music World to the notorious Waverly Hills Sanatorium, you'll read tales about hotels, schools, landmarks, graveyards, mountains, hills, tunnels, lonely roads, and many other locations including the historic Mammoth Cave. So if you're in for a good scare, sit back with the Frightening Floyds and learn all about Kentucky's Strange and Unusual Haunts.

BE OUR GHOST

by The Frightening Floyds

The Frightening Floyds invite you to be our ghost as we take you on a tour of the happiest haunted place on Earth! In this book, you will read about much of the alleged paranormal activity as well as some legends spanning the various Disney theme parks around the world. From the haunted dolls of It's a Small World to the real ghosts of the Haunted Mansion, there are many spirits here to greet you. And make sure to say "Good morning" to George at Pirates of the Caribbean. Enjoy the spooky and fascinating tales in Be Our Ghost! And don't worry, there are no hitchhiking ghosts ahead...or are there?

HANDBOOK FOR THE DEAD

DON'T FORGET YOUR HANDBOOK...Welcome all spirits! The Frightening Floyds present to you, Handbook for the Dead – a guide to help all new manifestations realize their functional perimeters. Within this anthology, you'll read paranormal accounts from individuals who have experienced phantoms and disturbances that have not only chilled them, but also left them with some new insight into the supernatural. Now, they want to share their stories and wisdom with you. That way, if you're feeling a little flat, or even if you're a lost soul, you won't have to draw a door and knock. Handbook for the Dead is sure to please the strange and unusual in everyone, and we promise it doesn't read like stereo instructions.

ALIENS OVER KENTUCKY

by The Frightening Floyds

F rom the Frightening Floyds, the pair of paranormal enthusiasts who brought you Be Our Ghost and Haunts of Hollywood Stars and Starlets comes a new adventure into the realm of the unknown – Aliens Over Kentucky. This collection includes the most noted extraterrestrial encounters from the Bluegrass State, such as the Kelly Creatures Incident of 1955, the Stanford Abductions, the Dogfight above General Electric, and the tale of Capt. Thomas Mantell chasing a UFO through Kentucky skies. But that's not all. There are lesser known, but equally intriguing, reports herein, such as the train collision with the UFO, stories of unexplained crop circles and cattle mutilations, Spring-heeled Jack, the Meat Shower of 1876, and many eyewitness reports of various unidentified crafts. You'll also read a couple of personal experiences from the authors, and even Muhammad Ali gets involved in the alien action. Join Jacob and Jenny Floyd as they dig into the mysterious cases and theories regarding Kentucky's "X-Files". Just be sure to keep one eye on the book and the other on the sky...

STRANGE AND UNUSUAL MYSTERIES

by The Frightening Floyds

What you are about to read is not a news report; it is neither a bulletin nor an alert. Rather, it is a collection of accounts of strange and unusual occurrences – some solved, some unsolved, but all mysterious. These reports have circulated for decades; some so much that they have become the sources of legends and rumors, even theories involving deep conspiracies. Despite many investigations and countless hours of research, there remain many questions unanswered. However, for every mystery there is someone out there who knows the truth, who possesses the evidence to solve the riddle. Maybe that someone will open this book and find their report. That someone could even be you.Ahead you will find tales of ghosts, missing persons, ancient legends, and extraterrestrial visitors. What are their stories, or, more importantly, where did their stories come from? Read the enclosed accounts and decide for yourself. Please, join us – maybe you can help the Frightening Floyds solve a mystery.

AMERICAN CRYPTIC

by Jim Towns

A MERICAN CRYPTIC is an open-minded cynic's take on the uncanny and sometimes frightening things which border our accepted reality. Through thirteen stories and essays, author and filmmaker Jim Towns examines several legends native to his own roots in Western Pennsylvania, and recalls some of his own unexplainable experiences as well. From legends of Native American giants buried under great earth mounds, to a haunted asylum, to a phantom trolley passenger, this work seeks not only to present the reader with new and fascinating supernatural tales, but also to deconstruct why our culture is so fascinated by their telling and re-telling.

PARANORMAL ENCOUNTERS

The Frightening Floyds present Paranormal Encounters: a collection of 14 tales of true ghostly experiences. From a malevolent spirit remaining in an apartment, to a loving phone call from a lost relative; from a house with a sliding chair and slamming doors, to a snow globe moving across a bedroom; from a possible past-life experience to a ghostly stranger in a radio station, this anthology contains several strange and unusual stories that are sure to entertain fans of the paranormal.

HAUNTS OF HOLLYWOOD STARS AND STARLETS

by The Frightening Floyds

Filmmakers, actors, actresses, comedians, writers, musicians—all have played their part in building the empire that is Hollywood. Many have legacies that are marred by controversy, mystery, and tragedy. But regardless of the scandals that followed these entertainers, they seem to inspire and influence moviegoers and television audiences all across the country; and because of this, they leave legacies that are not soon forgotten. But, not all of these artists and entertainers have simply left memories behind. According to different reports, there are some who allegedly haven't left at all. Many people have claimed to have seen the ghosts and spirits of some of these celebrities lingering in places they knew and loved in life. Jacob and Jenny Floyd, authors of Louisville's Strange and Unusual Haunts and Kentucky's Haunted Mansions, have researched some of these claims and compiled them for their latest book. Read Haunts of Hollywood Stars and Starlets to see if any of your favorites made the list.

READ MORE NIGHTMARE PRESS!!!

Thank you for reading!

For more great reads from Nightmare Press, check us out at: nightmarepress5.wordpress.com

Nightmare Press Facebook page
Nightmare Press Fans & Authors Facebook group
Instagram
Nightmare Press Network on YouTube

www.ingramcontent.com/pod-product-compliance
Lightning Source LLC
Chambersburg PA
CBHW021933040426
42448CB00008B/1049